Metamorphosis

Metamorphosis

A Poetry Collection

Aaron W. Poortvliet

XULON PRESS

Xulon Press
2301 Lucien Way #415
Maitland, FL 32751
407.339.4217
www.xulonpress.com

Paperback ISBN-13: 978-1-6628-3358-8

Dedicated to my grandmother,
Ivy Boren (1939-2018),
who was instrumental in the development
of my love for the English language.

Contents

D-Day

As he leaped from the meager gore-stained protection
Of the curse-riddled, wound-echoing Higgins boat,
Nightmare lead unzipped him from sternum to groin.
Reflexive genuflection in the knee-high angry surf
Brought a final slug to rest between his crossed eyes.
His organs, having gorged themselves on adrenaline,
Eased into the tepid embrace of the crimsoning tide.
He sighed, then prostrated himself in the French water,
Submitting at last to the siren call of death's caress.

Conniptions

I.

To the uninitiated, condemnation seems logical.
Creatives of any age who choose an early death
Are often targets of hostile, unwarranted criticism.
But gaze on their images; see the unifying feature:
The look of helpless infantility and willing madness
Mingled in measure on each one's fear-worn brow.
Their eyes plead with Percy Shelley's 'Ozymandias',
"Look on my Works, ye Mighty, and despair!"

II.

Was Hart Crane still attempting to outdo T. S. Eliot
When he leaped into the turquoise wine of the Gulf?
Still seeking to create a mystical synthesis of America?
When the *Orizaba*'s crewman refused his overtures,
Was it one straw too many for his overburdened soul,
Thus prompting him to imbibe the venomous alcohol?

Did Ernest Hemingway hear the bells tolling for him,
Or did he fancy himself a matador and his gun a bull
When death tore a hole in his head in the mountains
Of Hailey, Idaho, days before the nation's birthday?
Or were his final moments spent trying to equate
His mental troubles with Santiago's giant blue marlin?

Was Sylvia Plath seeking revenge against her husband
When she opened the gas valve and drank the vapors
That clouded her head early in the suicidal morning?
Were her final moments spent thinking of her children:
Of Frieda and Nicholas and the fact that she'd never

Again feel their arms wrap around her slender neck?

Was Randall Jarrell an actor as much as he was a poet?
He may have fooled many, including his second wife,
But friends, who like him had played with a cold fire,
Knew beyond doubt that he had not opened his hand
To the Herculean effort that would have been required
To beat the desire for death that led him to the highway.

As his feet left the glacial Washington Avenue Bridge
That January Minnesota morning, was John Berryman
Still thinking of possible additions for his *Dream Songs*?
Or was his mistress, the ethereal poet Anne Bradstreet
Whispering her 'Upon a Fit of Sickness, Anno. 1632'
In his ear as he descended with terminal determination?

Was Anne Sexton thinking of Comfort when she died—
Her grandfather and those friends she had so nicknamed—
Or was she fixated (as she had been for years) on Nana,
Her snuggling companion and confidante of childhood?
Did music swim back to her while she sipped iced vodka
As the garage transformed into her personal gas chamber?

Dylan Thomas understood the moment after he died
How wrong he had been to make the blanket statement
That "death shall have no dominion." His admonition,
"Do not go gentle into that good night," was ignored
By gout, cirrhosis, and lungs stained by warm nicotine,
Which combined to bear him away to Death's bosom
Only two weeks after he entered his thirty-ninth year.

When he fell asleep in the isolation of a New York taxi,

3

Robert Lowell at last escaped his tiring manic depression
And left behind his Puritan, Boston Brahmin ancestors.
Could it be that death at sixty was more bearable to him
Than embracing more insidious, unavoidable relapses?
Perhaps his subconscious transmuted into Lord Weary
So that he could inhabit a silent, solitary buried castle.

III.
Hope, despair, community, isolation—all intermingle
In the minds of poets, authors, and luminary critics alike.
Creativity and wordplay can be beautiful yet terrible,
Taskmasters that seduce without apology or reprieve,
Leaving their intoxicated, inspired victims witless.

Recurring Nightmare

It's always the same:
I sit alone at a cold, steel interrogation table.
A bare bulb hangs out of sight above me
Like a red dwarf star: invisible to the naked eye.
Out of the darkness, someone, faceless,
Approaches and places a loaded pistol
On the table before me.
As she walks away (yes, I can tell
By the figure that it's a she),
I put the gun to my head
And pull the trigger.
Nothing happens.
Again I pull the trigger.
Same result.
Then I wake up.

Death in the Trysting Place

He sat quaking in the perfumed heat of the crowded room,
Feeling not unlike a wet, ragged towel being twisted dry.
Terror, like a fiery flood tide coursing through his veins,
Spawned a growing damp spot between his jittering legs.
His constricted sandpit throat yearned for even a drop
Of warm water, bitter coffee, whiskey…anything liquid!
At only nineteen, it was legal for him to ride the lightning.
The chair of death was called "Old Sparky" by some;
"The Executioner" by others. He refused to smell
The electricity-steeped black hood that covered his face
Or the hot, metallic stench of the crimson ribbons
That had grinned across his parents' throats
After he'd murdered them while they slept.
He shrank from the malignant drool of the sponge
As it caressed his now clean-shaven crown.
His mind retreated to the memory of a barn loft,
Congested with fresh-baled timothy and alfalfa
That concealed a boy and girl, naked as newborns,
Doing little to muffle their newfound ecstasy.
As though from a distance, he heard a voice intone,
"Electricity shall now be passed through your body
Until you are dead. God have mercy on your soul."
Still entangled in his reverie, he little felt the volts
Jolting him into the anguished darkness from which
There was no hope of temporary reprieve or escape.

She sat mute, rigid, unaware of those around her,
Next to the closet that housed the spindle of death.
Murmurs of "Let 'im fry!" and "Roast 'im good!"
Pierced her mind and ears; brought a voiceless,

Tormented "No!" to her horror-whitened lips.
She heard the final condemnation and the fall
Of the death-hastening lever; watched in agony
As his short life juddered and grunted away.
Only when confirmation of death was given
Did she mingle with other departing spectators:
But one more body in a sea of abject strangers.
Slapped in the face by August's torpid breath,
She followed her watery shadow with dread
Toward a home she would never enter again.
A skylark's uninhibited anthem of praise
Brought unbidden tears of rage and despair.
Lurching, desperate, toward a familiar barn,
Once a trysting place for frenetic young lovers,
She hurried, stumbling, across the unlit bay
To an unprotesting, unconcerned ladder.
Twenty feet up, haunted by echoes of pleasure,
She knotted a willing rope around her throat,
Muttered a final farewell to the pungent air,
Then stepped, uncringing, off the platform,
Welcoming the sharp embrace of the drop.

Imaginings

Specters and phantoms of past misdeeds
Haunt my every miserable waking thought.
Hallucinatory and inanimate they may be,
But my constant companions nonetheless.
There was the geriatric I killed one day
For offering me the choice between
Injury and insult. I desired neither.
Or the young man I throttled that night
For attempting to proselytize my soul
Out of Hell. I am damned already!
These are but two of the faces I see,
Their voices intoning ceaseless diatribes
Of my own crazed mind's concoction...
The words sear like methanol flames:
Invisible, but no less a source of anguish.
Hell shall offer me no solace. Like Faust,
I must live with the results of my choices
For eternity, deplorable though they be.

Refusing Mr. Hyde

I sit beneath the ice-flecked fury of your eye,
Its incandescence threatening to consume me.
My resolve to deny you shrivels, but holds on.
You do not attack me. You have no need to.
Your presence alone drives me raving mad.
Why were you permitted access to my mind?

I will no longer do your bidding. I refuse it!
In truth, you are only a conjured aberration.
I have ogled you; I have even coddled you.
I will no longer cede to you all you might ask.
I can no longer be a slave to my imagination!
If this is madness in its fullness, it must be so.
I can, must and will be free of it at any cost!

Ruminations

Is it possible that I am only drunk on thoughts of suicide,
That my desire to end my life is nothing but a caricature?
Anxiety and serenity are convinced to be such fast friends
That they cohabitate with impunity in my wearied soul.
Odd though this union may seem to the confused passerby,
The alluring venom of each blends with its equal opposite,
Numbing my desire to embrace one and banish the other.

Depression

It stalks with agonizing persistence,
Drowning competing voices that whisper,
"Move on! Ignore the malignant shroud!
Embrace inevitable demise by any means!"

The agitated desire for life is often overcast
By the desperate urge to pursue its termination.
Logic is thus replaced by conniving longing
For forbidden, macabre methods of execution.

Like a child banished to the silent corner of rebuke,
Hope clings to its crumbling, razor-riddled toehold
On the soul held captive by the reeking exhalation:
A smog that welcomes the rapid dying of the light.

Bars of the Mind

The sunrise here offers little hope;
It is more painful than the midnight.
Shards of light pierce my taxed soul
Like cold acid applied to paper cuts.
Exuberant, joyful gloom glues itself
To my tissue paper-wrinkled brow.

I am trapped, seduced, by a prison
Of my own unsound mind's creation.
Though at first I found it hideous,
My tenure has effected comfortability.
Moreover, I am corrupted by docility,
Making me now unwilling to depart.

I spend each midday in a courtyard
Decorated by ice ivy and hoarfrost.
I lie naked, exposed to the elements,
Enduring the assault of frost flakes.
These tattoo themselves on my soul,
Ignoring my dull screams for mercy.

In the evenings, I sit dumb and deaf
On the edge of a porous basalt cliff,
Gazing across a tideless, silent sea
Toward the place where the red sun
Will claim its right to frigid rebirth
When the raving night is exhausted.

Job Interview

What kind of person are you? What kind of applicant?
You don't need to answer; they're rhetorical questions.

Tell me all about yourself in fewer than fifty words.
No, not your life story or your work history, you oaf!

You have fifteen years of experience in this line of work?
As fascinating as that might seem, it's not very relevant.

Can you do what you're told? Not ask stupid questions?
I can already see by the look on your face that you can't.

You seem very shifty to me; unable to focus, moreover.
Don't bother with an excuse; it'd be a waste of breath.

Do you feel off balance yet? Bored by rehearsed trivia?
I can see the glaze of my own eyes reflected in yours.

You know as well as I do that this is a waste of time.
I still have thirty more applicants I need to dishearten.

The cogs in your head look ready to grind to a standstill.
Do you have any pressing questions you want to ask?

No? Good. That makes both our jobs that much easier.
Oh, wait! Ha! I forgot that you don't even have a job!

I don't give a whit about your numerous aspirations.
Dreams, goals and skills will never land you a job.

Well, nice to meet you. We'll call you in a few days.
(Which, you understand, means you'll never be hired.)

Longing for Life

I never yearned for a bullet or a knife.
I could have made use of a noose, perhaps,
Though that still might have been difficult.
My desire was for a quick, painless end
That would not leave a mess for others.
But day by day my strength was renewed,
Even when I had made up my tired mind
That any given day would be my last.

I've proven myself faithless each day,
Yet the Lord has been faithful and true.
This lesson has been a challenge to learn:
That God's grace depends only on God.
If my salvation was left in my dirty hands,
I'd be wandering down a pointless road
Until death stole my opportunity for grace;
Until I was told, "Depart, I never knew you."

Migraine

It always starts in the submissive unconscious:
A dull throbbing that gutters like sadistic coals,
Then morphs into a remorseless, cyclonic beast
That beats its harsh tattoo into the fracturing skull.
Its tentacles cajole the arteries and veins to spasm;
Coax the eyes to submit to sublime vice-gripping
Till every atom of the head joins the chorus of pain.

Unhelpful Signs

I've often thought it odd that so many neighborhoods
Have signs warning drivers of the slow children at play.
Almost as bizarre are the signs about slow speed bumps.
Every speed bump I've ever seen has been stationary.
And regardless of whether children are slow or not,
Many drivers are crazy enough that they don't need
Any kind of incentive to chase down young innocents.

The Death of Conscience

Jink and Judder will always shudder
At the memory of the awful day
When Jiminy Cricket was devoured
By a merciless cat in the garden,
Leaving Pinocchio to run amok.

Edible Puzzles

No self-respecting five-year-old would find it amusing:
The Facebook meme of a package of smoked, diced ham
That someone labeled a 'Peppa Pig jigsaw puzzle'.

When pigs and cows are funneled into single-file lines,
Do they think they are going to a land of perpetual delight?
Or do they have an awareness that the puzzle pieces
That make up their bodies are about to be sundered forever:
Chopped, diced, ground, smoked and otherwise destroyed?
When metal bolts send them on that journey of no return,
Do they understand that the envenomed Prince of Denmark
Was right to say with his final breath, "The rest is silence"?

Ramblings

Have you ever seen the inside of my head?
One side is a glorified swimming pool
(Pool is loop written backward, you know).
And since the left side of my brain was removed,
I have been able to argue for twenty years
(With limited success, I will admit)
That I am forever and always in my right mind.
The remaining pound and a half of gray matter
Is an incongruous, eclectic assortment
Of facts most people find quite useless.
These are jumbled together with snippets
Of songs I remember from my childhood
And the words and phrases I've learned
In a dozen and a half disparate languages.
Then there are the names of twoscore poets:
The ones who courted depression for years
And those who chose to take their own lives
Have been the ones I've related to the best
(As unfortunate and unhelpful as that may be).
Leonardo Da Vinci designed flying machines…
Anne Sexton gassed herself in her garage…
Sometimes my brain won't stop whirling
From thought to unconnectable thought,
As though it's striving to wear me down.
I sometimes think that my body hates me:
Lancing migraines through my skull and eyes
Or gouging my rib cage with dull rapiers.
It is rare when I feel at home in my own body,
When we seem able to live in perfect harmony.

Confuzzlement

To be a fool I do not wish,
So I would never be a fish.
And yet, no wisdom is obtained
If all the fish in one pond are contained.
O humor me! I do insist!
Unless you wish to meet my fist!
That meeting here I have arranged,
Because, you see, I am deranged!
Since half a brain only have I to use,
My friends and foes I oft confuse.
This is not very good for me,
For friend and foe from me do flee.
I'll die an old and broken man
If through my head I stick a fan.

Rampage

Why the pastel pink- and yellow-stained plates
Kindled his disapproval he could never later say,
But their vile presence drove him to distraction.
Their cavalier relaxation in the china cabinet
Made his endless labor even more objectionable.

Their adopted impertinence spurred him to action
As the sun surrendered to the horizon's gravity,
Smudging the clouds death-mottled purple and red.

With feigned care, he placed his foes in a white box,
Which he carried to a window by his small balcony,
Itself crowded by brittle chrysanthemums and roses.
Raising the green-framed sixteen-squared pane,
He gazed on the smooth, glazed faces one last time.

Then, with the joyous, carefree grin of a besotted maniac,
He flung them like fragile frisbees into the moist air.
Some seemed to hover, uncertain, for a moment or two
Before shuddering toward the asphalt four stories below.
The rest arced toward their demise with seeming abandon,
Eager to complete the errand they had been launched on.

Rightful Unhappiness

There once was a man named Curmudgeon
Whom everyone wanted to bludgeon.
So Curmudgeon did flee
On a raft on the sea,
And lived for ten years in high dudgeon.

Restrained in the Psych Ward

Is this an interview? Or an interrogation?
Am I allowed to depart at my leisure?
Please remove these wrist and ankle restraints.
I can assure you that they are quite unnecessary.
Why are there no pictures on the walls here?
No Monets, Picassos, Da Vincis, or O'Keeffes?
Do you think it's somehow therapeutic to glare,
Eyes glazed over, at bland features all day?
Please, I beg you, remove these manacles.
I promise not to leave without permission…
Truth be told, I could escape this place faster
Than any of the doctors or nurses could say
'Subdermal hematoma' or 'dihydrogen monoxide'.
Again I beseech you: remove these chains.
Are you unable to see that I am subdued?
I am no threat to anyone, least of all myself.
Doctor? Doctor! Please? Please!
I have done nothing to deserve such treatment!
No, I would not like a dose or two of Valium.
And I have no use for a prescription for Xanax.
Are you blind?! I am meek and sedate already!
My hands and feet are starting to go numb!
They are being assaulted by bands of Velcro!
Relax? Relax?! I need to relax, you say?!
Of course I am hyperventilating,
You hen-pecking cow pie-faced buffoon!
I've been sitting here for hours
With only myself for company!
Doctor? Doctor! Please? Please!

The Death of Independent Thought

The ivy-burdened exteriors of higher education
Often serve as bright, ornamented sepulchers
For the lily-strewn corpses of personal agendas.
The liberty to form one's own opinion is gone,
Replaced by the 'group-think' Orwell imagined.
Too many among the so-called intellectual elite
Have built careers preying on blithe gullibility,
On taking advantage of those who were trained
From earliest youth to abhor critical thinking.
Self-education is no longer pushed or promoted,
And this detrimental concept has been accepted:
That the most profitable course anyone can take
Is to bow at the feet of 'subject matter experts'.

Aerobatics Pilot

He cavorted and tumbled into the borderless azure dome,
The ruby wings of his plane an extension of his own body.
Racing through bales of washed-sheep cumulus clouds,
He glanced below to appreciate the fence-stitched fields
That marched to the horizon in emerald and amber hues.
Then, like a lone tern in pursuit of a school of mackerel,
He stooped and corkscrewed toward the nattering crowd.
Two hundred feet above the swarm of cloches and fedoras,
He brought the stick back and flaps up, launching skyward,
The earth whirling away behind his Curtiss JN-4 'Jenny'.
A mile and a half into the emptiness, he killed the engine;
Allowed himself to plunge: a meteorite high on adrenaline.
At nine hundred feet he flipped the switch to ON again.
Nothing happened. He toggled it again. Same rude result.
Six hundred more feet bled away beneath his wings.
He shuddered; tried it one more time. The engine roared,
Drowning the fear screaming like a banshee in his ears.
Once more he raced through the vast void he loved.
Seeing that he was now riding on little more than fumes,
He descended for good with a familiar feeling of regret.

On Reading

Crack the cover and vanish for an hour (or five);
Submit to the inescapable draw of other worlds.
Consider the heart-arresting truths of Scripture:
The complex simplicity of God's salvation plan
That runs from Adam's sin to Christ's victory.
Take a few days to absorb the constructed myths
Of the vast Middle-Earth or the humbler Narnia.
Detail-dense volumes of multifaceted history
Demand and invite reflection and self-appraisal.
Biographies allow us unique access to the lives
Of the rich and famous and of the obscure alike.
Follow and observe the growth of the exploits
Of Alexander the Great and Napoleon Bonaparte;
Marvel at the humility of Dietrich Bonhoeffer;
Learn from the self-abasement of St. Augustine.
From T. S. Eliot to Robert Frost to Anne Sexton,
Poets explore the broad depths of our existence
And give corporeality to great pain and deep joy.
Time and space lose immediacy as bold creativity,
Freed of visual encumbrances, wields its power.
Only when the grudging book cover snaps shut
Do weight and the body's boundaries crash in,
Once more infringing on freedoms of the mind.

Death at Either End

I saw a beetle marching on a log one day,
His steps sure as he moved from end to end.
He seemed unaware of the orange curtains
That were eating away his world. Intrigued,
I watched to see whether the bleak futility
Of his solitary parade would dawn on him.
All the while, the ravenous heat encroached
Ever further on the island beneath his feet.
As flames caressed his twitching carapace,
He turned in a few seconds to a pile of ash.

Aerial Battles

Have you ever observed feathered fighter planes
Swooping and circling around robber bombers,
Risking their own lives to protect the young
Inexperienced soldiers in the sniperless nests?

The Water Skate's Demise

He skittered across the swift-flowing liquid crystal,
Creating haphazard dimples in its mirroring surface.
A pale, overcast eye observed him without malice,
For a time withholding its temperamental cold fury.
He journeyed on, unaware of the curious danger
Watching his every move from the cover of silence.

The hook-festooned maw, proof of determination
To cheat death many times, vised open and shut.
Dead eyes, lit by hunger and rabid self-preservation,
Tracked the tasty morsel jigging its death dance
On the light-spangled surface above. Launching
Into motion, no bubble traitored the fish's approach.

He found himself jerked beneath the watery shroud,
Promised heaven replaced with actualized purgatory.
He thrashed to no avail at the face of his assailant.
Negligence and inattentiveness had been his undoing.
As the jaws of death clamped down, he discovered:
Death unprepared for remains death just the same.

Pancakes

It seems an odd choice of location for a nap,
And as many squirrels discover far too late,
There's no waking up from a careless snooze
Between white and yellow lines and the curb.

The Bird

On naked bough
In winter storm,
There sat a ruby
Cardinal.

The Perspective of the Fly

Have you ever considered the perspective of the fly
Who sits upon your wall and rubs his tiny legs together?
How the world must look through his small eyes?
Things we think are small must seem gargantuan to him.
No wonder: that he zooms away each time we raise a hand.
He must live in perpetual fear of being crushed.
After all, he's only got a short twenty-four hours
To do whatever it is a fly does with its life.

By the Pond

The echoes of rain:
A bullfrog reminisces
On his recent bath.

No Need to Fear

Silent Sunday shadows were lengthening
As a man walked with his young daughter,
Their entwined fingers a demonstration
Of their reciprocal, unflagging love.
They turned down a gloomed wooded path,
Only to reach a dead end minutes later.
As they turned to retrace their steps,
The man asked, "Are you scared?"
"Oh, no, Papa," the girl replied, unhesitating.
"As long as you walk with me and hold my hand,
I don't ever have to be scared."

Remembrances

I brush rusty leaves away;
Bare a polished marble slab:
Sylvia Marie Bradstreet
May 10th, 1921
to June 13th, 2012
My eyes see dark carved letters;
My mind sees only her face.

§§§

We met at a church picnic
December 6th, '41,
The day before Pearl Harbor.
Four months later, I became
An Army Air Corps pilot.
I told her, "Please wait for me,"
The day I left for Europe.

§§§

Her notes were always hopeful,
Encouraging and vivid.
My Bible and her letters
Gave me resolve for each day
And strength for every mission
As my crew bombed Germany
From Hanover to Berlin.

§§§

"Jerries!" I heard someone scream
As swastikas dove upward.
Then I felt, or rather watched,

Silver shrapnel pierce my leg.
As death swirled around my plane,
My mind entered a bleak fog
As I fought to stay alive.

§§§

With a chest full of medals
And a slight limp, I went home.
We married four months later,
Then started a family.
I learned to service airplanes;
She became a homemaker.
Together, we raised four kids.

§§§

Her hair grew gray, then silver;
Mine, receded, turned snow white.
Age proved very kind to us:
She'd sit crocheting for hours,
While I practiced woodcarving.
Jeopardy! kept our minds sharp
As our bodies grew more frail.

§§§

Then one day, she fell asleep
And woke in another world.
For sixty-eight golden years
She had been my companion,
My one and only helpmate.
My daughter cares for me now,
And my sons often visit.

§§§

I brush rusty leaves away;
Bare a polished marble slab:
Sylvia Marie Bradstreet
May 10th, 1921
to June 13th, 2012
My eyes see dark carved letters;
My mind sees her in Heaven.

Farewell, My Child

We dug you a two-by-three foot plot in the garden today;
In the blessed presence of the Savior you may now rejoice.
Pink crepe myrtles and roses whispered a perfumed lullaby,
Their tears patterning a warm shroud o'er new-turned earth.

O my heart's delight! Your pain and toil are now complete.
I must carry on alone. Please greet your mother for me…
I would do so myself, but I must tarry here awhile longer
To tend the sorrow-dappled beds of the flowers I have lost.

Weed Pulling

There are so many varieties: some are hideous;
Others display pleasing flowers and perfumes.
But they must all see themselves as beautiful,
Or they would be more congenial to removal.
Some have unobtrusive inch-deep root systems,
But some of their neighbors are more tenacious,
Having single roots that plunge ten inches deep.
Clearing the plot from the grip of the green fiends
Can be back-straining and patience-whittling.
Even the most determined person can wind up
Ready to hurl a hoe at the uncooperative plants.

Like the weeds, the innumerable sins we caress
Seem unwilling to be uprooted and discarded.
But the Gardener of our souls is ever-patient,
Replacing our favorite, cherished wrongdoings
With righteousness that will grow and endure.
Though his careful ministrations seem painful,
We find in time that his surgery proves healing.
When he cuts away wickedness in its infancy,
We discover that we are saved the heartache
That deep-rooted sin causes us and often others.
Then we are freed to rejoice in his tender care.

Pride and Humility

Muttering a song of ascents devoid of conviction,
He strode into the temple's crowded court to pray.
Brushing imagined dust motes from his tassels,
The Pharisee raised his proud eyes toward heaven,
Thundering in a voice that commanded attention,
"God, I thank you that I am not like other men—
Robbers, evildoers, adulterers—" He paused
To glance at those surrounding him, then sneered.
"I thank you that I am not like this man here…
This *tax collector*," he spat with bile. "I fast
Twice a week and give a tenth of all my gain
To the poor." Still self-absorbed, he walked away
Through the crowd, bound to many obligations,
Incapable of repentance or a desire to change.

He knew that many viewed him as a turncoat,
That others saw him as a pet of the hated Romans.
Like the Pharisee, he had come to pray out of duty,
But the bitter indictment had pierced his heart
And drawn sincerity from the recesses of his soul.
Kneeling, he would not even lift his closed eyes
Toward heaven, but beat his chest, whispering,
"God, have mercy on me, a sinful, unholy man."
He ignored the murmurs of those around him;
Paid no heed to the hushed rebuke and derision.
Buoyed by peace he had never experienced before,
He rose and departed with a new song in his heart,
Rejoicing in the gift of freedom and forgiveness
That had been poured into his soul by a loving God.

Welcomed to the Table

I am unworthy to even beg for scraps at his gate,
Yet he brought me to his royal banqueting table
And from it gave me more than I could conceive.
His banner over me is unmerited, undeserved love.
I take my refuge in the healing shade of his wing;
He himself guards my lying down and my rising.
Even when hosts of enemies encircle my camp,
He prepares a feast to sate the longings of my soul.
My horn is lifted up and my head anointed with oil.

The Day of Salvation

"Be still and know that I am God," says the Lord of Hosts.
"I will be exalted by every tongue in Heaven and on earth;
By those the earth consumes I will be held in reverence."
Praise the Lord with trembling, you servants of the King!
Raise a thunderous anthem of joy, you who see his face!
Today is the day of salvation; tomorrow is not guaranteed.

O foolish generation! Open your stopped ears and hearts!
Do not say in arrogance, "The Lord takes no notice of us."
The wrath of God is revealed against all unrighteousness;
Is unleashed on all who fail to call upon his holy name.

Only the fool says in his stubborn heart, "There is no God."
Only a dullard maintains such an untenable perspective.
Their conceited disdain for obvious truth is their downfall,
And though the Lord will find no pleasure in their deaths,
He will not withhold due judgment on the appointed day.

Therefore, worship the mighty King with reverent humility;
Accept the proffered position as his blessed servant-child.
Give thanks for the salvation Christ wrought on our behalf:
The bounteous gift of eternal life we could never afford.
Raise thundering anthems of praise to the King of all kings!

The Obedience of Christ

As great drops of bloody sweat fell from his brow
Beneath the moonlit olive trees of quiet Gethsemane,
It was not fear of the whip or the cruel iron spikes
Which caused the bitterness and anguish in his soul,
Though he understood that he must soon endure these.
Neither was it the jeering of the Jewish leaders,
Nor the falling away of his twelve closest friends.
Rather, it was the moment when the Father
Would turn his face away that he dreaded the most.

"Yet, Father, not my will but yours be done."

He endured the malicious kiss of his betrayer,
Yet knocked the leering crowd to the ground
With the words, "I have told you that I am he,"
And took a moment to reattach Malchus's ear.
As he hung naked and exposed on the cross,
He cried out, "Father, forgive them,
For they know not what they are doing."
And when the moment of separation came,
He screamed, "Eloi, Eloi, lama sabachthani?!"

"Yes, Father, for this was your good pleasure."

As he strove to fill his tortured, aching lungs,
He gasped, "Father, into your hands I commit
My spirit." His body went rigid as it sagged,
And the light in his eyes faded and went out.
"Surely this man was the Son of God,"
Said the centurion in charge of the execution.

Three days later, in the tomb of a rich man,
Life reentered the body of the Son of Man.
With a word, he rolled the sealed stone away.

"All authority…has been given to me."

For forty days he revealed himself to many:
He reinstated one who had thrice denied him;
Rebuked one who had doubted his resurrection.
He walked with downcast men toward Emmaus,
Ate with them, then vanished from their sight.
He appeared to over five hundred at one time;
Laid the foundations for the birth of the church.
When the time came for him to return to Heaven,
He said to those gathered on the Mount of Olives,

"Lo, I am with you always: to the end of the age."

The Chief of Sinners

I know myself too well to be able to confess any less:
I am the two-faced chief of sinners. Some would argue
That such could never be the case, and to some degree,
I would be forced to agree with their bold reassurances.

I cannot, will not do it! I must name myself the worst!
There cannot be any creature more vile or conniving.
I would with unfettered gladness carve from my chest
This fickle heart of granite that rattles against my ribs.

With it, I have worshiped many created things
Rather than the Creator, who alone is deserving
Of the praise I would render with every breath:
My confession, my adoration and thanksgiving.

I have used the name of God in many ways
That it should never be slandered or abused.
And though I rail against others who do this,
I brush aside my own sin with little thought.

I have desired things forbidden by a holy God,
Fantasized about fornication and unlawfulness.
My sin is no less an abomination than David's,
Nor is it lacking in horror compared to Amnon's.

I am guilty of looking with calculating jealousy
On the gilded possessions of those around me;
I have coveted things that are not mine to have,
As Ahab desired to claim the vineyard of Nabal.

O Lord my God! How can you still love me?
Even as I confess these innumerable wrongs,
I find newborn faults and fresh abominations
In the fertile soil of my self-destructive heart.

Yet to this, my hope and joy, I hold and cling:
The blood of Christ has purchased my pardon,
Has made me blameless in the Father's sight
So that I may dwell with him for all eternity.

Eternal Praise

I have treasured your Word in my heart, O God,
That I might not be guilty of repulsive, willful sin.
Set a guard over my heart and my mind, O Lord,
For I know the wickedness of which each is capable.
Let me not glory in my knowledge and understanding,
But revel in your wisdom alone, O my righteous King.

I have been washed in the blood of Christ my Savior,
The Lamb of God who takes away the sins of the world.
I can only kneel, staggered by his awesome presence:
Struck dumb by the holy beauty of his amazing grace.
Even when eternity has passed into boundless eternity,
I will use every breath to praise the God of my salvation.

Comforters

How do you help when you don't know what to say?
How do you reach a friend who can't escape the fog?
Give him the gift of presence. Offer to watch her kids.
You don't need to have an answer for every question,
But don't be afraid to make some queries of your own.
Invite him to engage in a study of Job's trials with you;
Offer to meet with her for lunch one day each week.
Listen for cues like, "I'm so tired," or "What's the use?"
If you hear something worrisome, don't just brush it off.
When he resists your efforts to make conversation, pray.
If she says she's tired of talking, take a walk together.
Read and study Scripture for your own spiritual benefit.
Then the peace of God, which passes all understanding,
Can be shared to ease the burdens your friend is facing.

There is a Friend who sticks closer than any brother,
Who prayed in the olive grove, "Not my will, Father,
But yours be done," knowing the agony that lay ahead.
He himself bore our sins in his own body on the tree.
More than any earth-bound counselor or comforter,
He understands our brokenness and our desperation,
For he knows us better than we can know ourselves.
Nor is he an aloof dictator who watches us from afar.
Rather, he came to this dark world to dwell among us,
Was tempted in every way yet remained pure and sinless.
His name is Wonderful Counselor and Mighty God,
Everlasting Father, the awesome Prince of Peace.
He tells us that in this life we will have trouble,
But that the joy of eternity is as sure as tomorrow.

Willing Sacrifice

In the wisdom and sovereign will of Almighty God,
We were raised up and saved for such a time as this:
That we might stand in the stunning grip of his grace.
We were rescued from the vile slave market of sin;
The vicarious life, death and resurrection of Christ
Purchased our eternal pardon from the grave's curse.
His priceless blood, shed on the cross, paid the debt
That a mountain of good deeds could never appease.
Therefore, we pour out our thankful praise each day
As we search our fickle hearts moment by moment
For self-serving, thronging indulgences to sacrifice.
We cannot forget that our bodies are temples of God,
Not to be abused by momentary, fleeting pleasure,
But devoted to the service of the holy King of kings.
The Lord has placed eternity in the hearts of all men
So that no man may claim ignorance or innocence.
Scripture is thereby proven accurate and infallible,
And on the day of final judgment, all men will bow,
And every humbled tongue in Heaven and on earth,
Together with those that were consigned to the grave,
Will confess at last that Jesus Christ alone is Lord
To the praise and awesome glory of God the Father.

Brief Acquaintance

Death, be not proud when you meet the souls
Of those redeemed by the blood of the Lamb,
Christ Jesus, who takes away the sins of men
Who seek him and name him their 'All in All',
For your power over them lasts but a moment.

The Gleam of Glory

She stepped from this life into the next with joy.
Escaping the austere quiet of the hospital room,
She received an exuberant chorus of greetings
From assembled friends, familiar and soon-to-be.
Her breath caught at the holy brilliance of Charis,
That home she had longed for years to glimpse.
She found the unadulterated oxygen of Heaven
Intoxicating, like a stream of crystal-pure water.
Beckoned to pass beyond the pearlescent gates,
She paused to gape at the boundless panoramas:
The visions of rapture that now burst on her sight.
Feeling a pair of hands squeezing her shoulders,
She spun around with a dazzling grin of delight
To behold the Ancient of Days, the Lamb of God,
Who stood prepared to embrace her in welcome.
She found herself swept up in the air like a child,
Willing, longing, to gaze into his eyes for an age.
Set down at last, she knelt, silenced by wonder
At the horrific scars in his ankles and wrists.
All else faded around her as she at last beheld
The glory gleam from eternal wounds of grace
And heard the welcome, "Well done, my child,
My good and faithful servant! Enter into my joy,
Into this home designed and prepared for you!"

Final Entreaty

Today I count this life as past;
Now death may blink my eyes at last.
Eternity bursts on my sight
As glory-bound I wing my flight.

Friends! Mourn me not this happy day,
For I've escaped the tiring fray!
Rejoice for me, for I am home;
At last I've entered Heaven's dome.

CPSIA information can be obtained
at www.ICGtesting.com
Printed in the USA
LVHW050122181121
703621LV00015BA/565